Rubáiyát of Omar Khayyám

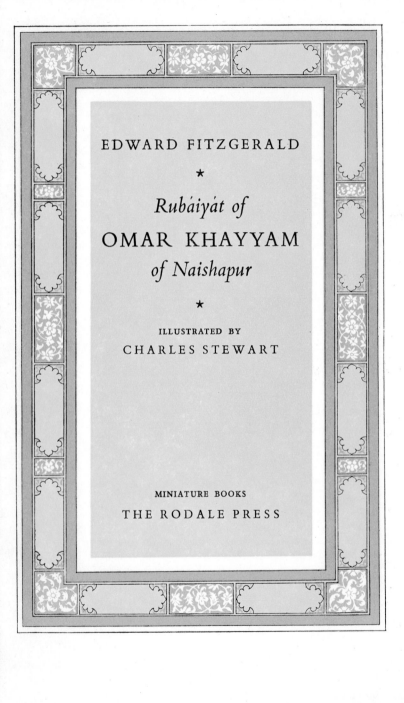

EDWARD FITZGERALD

★

Rubáiyát of
OMAR KHAYYAM
of Naishapur

★

ILLUSTRATED BY
CHARLES STEWART

MINIATURE BOOKS
THE RODALE PRESS

PUBLISHED IN 1955
BY THE RODALE PRESS
123 NEW BOND STREET, LONDON, W.I
AND BY RODALE BOOKS INC.
EMMAUS, PENNSYLVANIA
PRINTED AND BOUND IN ENGLAND
BY MACKAYS OF CHATHAM

NOTE

Since its first appearance, almost unnoticed, in 1859 Edward FitzGerald's brilliant paraphrase of the *Rubáiyát* of the twelfth century Persian poet Omar Khayyám has established itself as a masterpiece of English letters.

The quatrain known as a *rubái*—*rubáiyát* is the plural—was a favourite form in Persian poetry. It was intended to stand on its own; a brief, complete epigram in verse. FitzGerald, working from the manuscript in the Bodleian Library, selected *rubáiyát* at will and wove them into a continuous poem of seventy-five quatrains. He did not pretend that this was a literal translation: about half of the seventy-five were more or less direct renderings of Omar's *rubáiyát* and the others were combinations of several *rubáiyát* or came from the works of other poets.

The success of FitzGerald's work brought Omar Khayyám himself in for considerable critical scrutiny. Successive scholars denied his authorship of more and more of the *rubáiyát* once attributed to him and until recently his stock had fallen very low. But the discovery of new manuscripts within the last few years has restored Omar to his rightful place as a considerable figure in Persian poetry.

FitzGerald prepared five editions each differing from its predecessor. The first edition has been followed here; in it FitzGerald gave the title *Kúza Náma*—Book of Pots—to stanzas 59–66, and finished his book with the words *Tamám Shud*—The Very End.

❧ RUBÁIYÁT ❧

1

Awake! for Morning in the Bowl of Night
Has flung the Stone that puts the Stars to Flight:
And Lo! the Hunter of the East has caught
The Sultán's Turret in a Noose of Light.

2

Dreaming when Dawn's Left Hand was in the Sky
I heard a Voice within the Tavern cry,
'Awake, my Little ones, and fill the Cup
Before Life's Liquor in its Cup be dry.'

3

And, as the Cock crew, those who stood before
The Tavern shouted—'Open then the Door!
You know how little while we have to stay,
And, once departed, may return no more.'

4

Now the New Year reviving old Desires,
The thoughtful Soul to Solitude retires,
    Where the 'White Hand of Moses' on the Bough
Puts out, and Jesus from the Ground suspires.

5

Irám indeed is gone with all its Rose,
And Jamshyd's Sev'n-ring'd Cup where no one knows;
    But still the Vine her ancient Ruby yields,
And still a Garden by the Water blows.

6

And David's Lips are lock't; but in divine
High piping Péhlevi, with 'Wine! Wine! Wine!
    Red Wine!'—the Nightingale cries to the Rose
That yellow Cheek of hers to incarnadine.

7

Come, fill the Cup, and in the Fire of Spring
The Winter Garment of Repentance fling:
    The Bird of Time has but a little way
To fly—and Lo! the Bird is on the Wing.

And look—a thousand Blossoms with the Day
Woke—and a thousand scatter'd into Clay:
  And this first Summer Month that brings the Rose
Shall take Jamshýd and Kaikobád away.

But come with old Khayyám, and leave the Lot
Of Kaikobád and Kaikhosrú forgot:
  Let Rustum lay about him as he will,
Or Hátim Tai cry Supper—heed them not.

With me along some Strip of Herbage strown
That just divides the desert from the sown,
  Where name of Slave and Sultán scarce is known,
And pity Sultán Máhmúd on his Throne.

Here with a Loaf of Bread beneath the Bough,
A Flask of Wine, a Book of Verse—and Thou
  Beside me singing in the Wilderness—
And Wilderness is Paradise enow.

'How sweet is mortal Sovranty!'—think some:
Others—'How blest the Paradise to come!'
    Ah, take the Cash in hand and wave the Rest;
Oh, the brave Music of a distant Drum!

Look to the Rose that blows about us—'Lo,
Laughing,' she says, 'into the World I blow:
    At once the silken Tassel of my Purse
Tear, and its Treasure on the Garden throw.'

The Worldly Hope men set their Hearts upon
Turns Ashes—or it prospers; and anon,
    Like Snow upon the Desert's dusty Face
Lighting a little Hour or two—is gone.

And those who husbanded the Golden Grain'
And those who flung it to the Winds like Rain,
    Alike to no such aureate Earth are turn'd
As, buried once, Men want dug up again.

16

Think, in this batter'd Caravanserai
Whose doorways are alternate Night and Day,
    How Sultán after Sultán with his Pomp
Abode his Hour or two, and went his way.

17

They say the Lion and the Lizard keep
The Courts where Jamshýd gloried and drank deep:
    And Bahrám, that great Hunter—the Wild Ass
Stamps o'er his Head, and he lies fast asleep.

18

I sometimes think that never blows so red
The Rose as where some buried Caesar bled;
    That every Hyacinth the Garden wears
Dropt in its Lap from some once lovely Head.

19

And this delightful Herb whose tender Green
Fledges the River's Lip on which we lean—
    Ah, lean upon it lightly! for who knows
From what once lovely Lip it springs unseen!

Ah, my Belovéd, fill the Cup that clears
'To-day' of past Regrets and future Fears—
    'To-morrow'? Why, To-morrow I may be
Myself with Yesterday's Sev'n Thousand Years.

Lo! some we loved, the loveliest and best
That Time and Fate of all their Vintage prest,
    Have drunk their Cup a Round or two before
And one by one crept silently to Rest.

And we, that now make merry in the Room
They left, and Summer dresses in new Bloom,
    Ourselves must we beneath the Couch of Earth
Descend, ourselves to make a Couch—for whom?

Ah, make the most of what we yet may spend.
Before we too into the Dust descend;
    Dust into Dust, and under Dust, to lie,
Sans Wine, sans Song, sans Singer, and—sans End!

Alike for those who for 'To-day' prepare,
And those that after a 'To-morrow' stare,
    A Muezzín from the Tower of Darkness cries
'Fools! your Reward is neither Here nor There!'

Why, all the Saints and Sages who discuss'd
Of the Two Worlds so learnedly, are thrust
    Like foolish Prophets forth; their Words to Scorn
Are scatter'd, and their Mouths are stopt with Dust.

Oh, come with old Khayyám, and leave the Wise
To talk; one thing is certain, that Life flies;
    One thing is certain, and the Rest is Lies;
The Flower that once has blown for ever dies.

Myself when young did eagerly frequent
Doctor and Saint, and heard great Argument
    About it and about: but evermore
Came out by the same Door as in I went.

28

With them the Seed of Wisdom did I sow,
And with my own hand labour'd it to grow:
  And this was all the Harvest that I reap'd—
'I came like Water, and like Wind I go.'

29

Into this Universe, and 'why' not knowing,
Nor 'whence', like Water willy-nilly flowing:
  And out of it, as Wind along the Waste,
I know not 'whither', willy-nilly blowing.

30

What, without asking, hither hurried whence?
And, without asking, whither hurried hence!
  Another and another Cup to drown
The Memory of this Impertinence!

31

Up from Earth's Centre through the Seventh Gate
I rose, and on the Throne of Saturn sate,
  And many Knots unravel'd by the Road;
But not the Knot of Human Death and Fate.

There was a Door to which I found no Key:
There was a Veil past which I could not see:
    Some little Talk awhile of 'Me' and 'Thee'
There seemed—and then no more of 'Thee' and 'Me'.

Then to the rolling Heav'n itself I cried,
Asking, 'What Lamp had Destiny to guide
    Her little Children stumbling in the Dark?'
And—'A blind Understanding!' Heav'n replied.

Then to this earthen Bowl did I adjourn
My Lip the secret Well of Life to learn:
    And Lip to Lip it murmur'd—'While you live
Drink! for once dead you never shall return.'

I think the Vessel, that with fugitive
Articulation answer'd, once did live'
    And merry-make; and the cold Lip I kiss'd
How many Kisses might it take—and give!

36

For in the Market-place, one Dusk of Day,
I watch'd the Potter thumping his wet Clay:
   And with its all obliterated Tongue
It murmur'd—'Gently, Brother, gently, pray!'

37

Ah, fill the Cup:—what boots it to repeat
How Time is slipping underneath our Feet:
   Unborn 'To-morrow,' and dead 'Yesterday',
Why fret about them if 'To-day' be sweet!

38

One Moment in Annihilation's Waste,
One Moment, of the Well of Life to taste—
   The Stars are setting and the Caravan
Starts for the Dawn of Nothing—Oh, make haste!

39

How long, how long, in infinite Pursuit
Of This and That endeavour and dispute?
   Better be merry with the fruitful Grape
Than sadden after none, or bitter, Fruit.

40

You know, my Friends, how long since in my House
For a new Marriage I did make Carouse:
   Divorced old barren Reason from my Bed,
And took the Daughter of the Vine to Spouse.

41

For 'Is' and 'Is-not' though with Rule and Line,
And 'Up-and-down' without, I could define,
   I yet in all I only cared to know,
Was never deep in anything but—Wine.

42

And lately, by the Tavern Door agape,
Came stealing through the Dusk an Angel Shape
   Bearing a Vessel on his Shoulder; and
He bid me taste of it; and 'twas—the Grape!

43

The Grape that can with Logic absolute
The Two-and-Seventy jarring Sects confute:
   The subtle Alchemist that in a Trice
Life's leaden Metal into Gold transmute.

44

The mighty Mahmúd, the victorious Lord,
That all the misbelieving and black Horde
   Of Fears and Sorrows that infest the Soul
Scatters and slays with his enchanted Sword.

45

But leave the Wise to wrangle, and with me
The Quarrel of the Universe let be:
   And, in some corner of the Hubbub coucht,
Make Game of that which makes as much of Thee.

46

For in and out, above, about, below,
'Tis nothing but a Magic Shadow-show,
   Play'd in a Box whose Candle is the Sun,
Round which we Phantom Figures come and go.

47

And if the Wine you drink, the Lip you press,
End in the Nothing all Things end in—Yes—
   Then fancy while Thou art, Thou art but what
Thou shalt be—Nothing—Thou shalt not be less.

While the Rose blows along the River Brink,
With old Khayyám the Ruby Vintage drink:
  And when the Angel with his darker Draught
Draws up to Thee—take that, and do not shrink.

'Tis all a Chequer-board of Nights and Days
Where Destiny with Men for Pieces plays:
  Hither and thither moves, and mates, and slays,
And one by one back in the Closet lays.

The Ball no Question makes of Ayes and Noes,
But Right or Left as strikes the Player goes;
  And He that toss'd Thee down into the Field,
He knows about it all—HE knows—HE knows!

The Moving Finger writes; and, having writ,
Moves on: nor all thy Piety nor Wit
  Shall lure it back to cancel half a Line,
Nor all thy Tears wash out a Word of it.

And that inverted Bowl we call The Sky,
Whereunder crawling coop't we live and die,
  Lift not thy hands to 'It' for help—for It
Rolls impotently on as Thou or I.

With Earth's first Clay They did the Last Man's
    knead,
And then of the Last Harvest sow'd the Seed:
  Yea, the first Morning of Creation wrote
What the Last Dawn of Reckoning shall read.

I tell Thee this—When, starting from the Goal,
Over the shoulders of the flaming Foal
  Of Heav'n Parwín and Mushtara they flung,
In my predestin'd Plot of Dust and Soul.

The Vine had struck a Fibre; which about
If clings my Being—let the Súfi flout;
  Of my Base Metal may be filed a Key,
That shall unlock the Door he howls without.

And this I know: whether the one True Light,
Kindle to Love, or Wrath consume me quite,
*   One Glimpse of it within the Tavern caught*
Better than in the Temple lost outright.

Oh Thou, who didst with Pitfall and with Gin
Beset the Road I was to wander in,
*   Thou wilt not with Predestination round*
Enmesh me, and impute my Fall to Sin?

Oh, Thou, who Man of baser Earth didst make,
And who with Eden didst devise the Snake;
*   For all the Sin wherewith the Face of Man*
Is blacken'd Man's Forgiveness give—and take!

★

59

Listen again. One Evening at the Close
Of Ramazán, ere the better Moon arose,
  In that old Potter's Shop I stood alone
With the clay Population round in Rows.

60

And, strange to tell, among that Earthen Lot
Some could articulate, while others not:
  And suddenly one more impatient cried—
'Who is the Potter, pray, and who the Pot?'

61

Then said another—'Surely not in vain
My Substance from the common Earth was ta'en,
  That He who subtly wrought me into Shape
Should stamp me back to common Earth again.'

Another said—'Why, ne'er a peevish Boy,
Would break the Bowl from which he drank in Joy;
  Shall He that made the Vessel in pure Love
And Fancy, in an after Rage destroy!'

None answer'd this; but after Silence spake
A Vessel of a more ungainly Make:
  'They sneer at me for leaning all awry;
What! did the Hand then of the Potter shake?'

Said one—'Folks of a surly Tapster tell'
And daub his Visage with the Smoke of Hell;
  They talk of some strict Testing of us—Pish!
He's a Good Fellow, and 'twill all be well.'

Then said another with a long-drawn Sigh,
'My Clay with long oblivion is gone dry:
  But, fill me with the old familiar Juice,
Methinks I might recover by-and-bye!'

66

So while the Vessels one by one were speaking,
One spied the little Crescent all were seeking:
   And then they jogg'd each other, 'Brother! Brother!
Hark to the Porter's Shoulder-knot a-creaking!'

*

67

Ah, with the Grape my fading Life provide,
And wash my Body whence the Life has died,
   And in a Windingsheet of Vine-leaf wrapt
So bury me by some sweet Garden-side.

68

That ev'n my buried Ashes such a Snare
Of Perfume shall fling up into the Air
   As not a True Believer passing by
But shall be overtaken unaware.

Indeed the Idols I have loved so long
Have done my Credit in Men's Eye much wrong;
  Have drown'd my Honour in a shallow Cup,
And sold my Reputation for a Song.

Indeed, indeed, Repentance oft before
I swore—but was I sober when I swore?
  And then and then came Spring, and Rose-in-hand
My thread-bare Penitence apieces tore.

And much as Wine has play'd the Infidel,
And robb'd me of my Robe of Honour—well,
  I often wonder what the Vintners buy
One half so precious as the Goods they sell.

Alas, that Spring should vanish with the Rose!
That Youth's sweet-scented Manuscript should close!
  The Nightingale that in the Branches sang,
Ah, whence, and whither flown again, who knows!

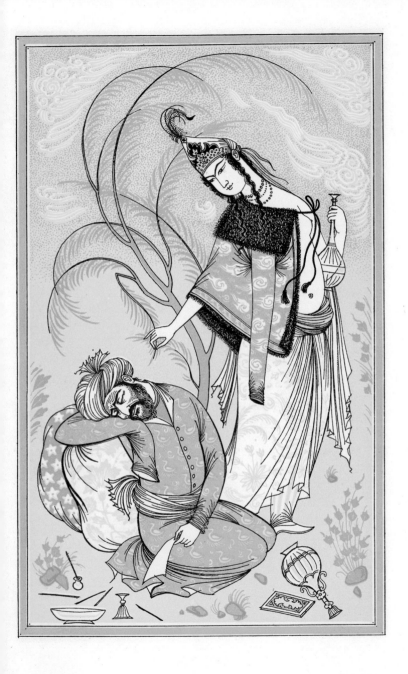

73

Ah Love! could thou and I with Fate conspire
To grasp this sorry Scheme of Things entire,
    Would not we shatter it to bits—and then
Re-mould it nearer to the Heart's Desire!

74

Ah, Moon of my Delight who know'st no wane,
The Moon of Heav'n is rising once again:
    How oft hereafter rising shall she look
Through this same Garden after me—in vain!

75

And when Thyself with shining Foot shall pass
Among the Guests Star-scatter'd on the Grass,
    And in thy joyous Errand reach the Spot
Where I made one—turn down an empty Glass.

TAMÁM SHUD